AF769689

My Struggle with Anorexia

Anne Gurberg

PublishAmerica
Baltimore

First printing

ISBN: 1-4241-2067-5
PUBLISHED BY PUBLISHAMERICA, LLLP
www.publishamerica.com
Baltimore

Printed in the United States of America

My Struggle with

Anorexia

Introduction

I am writing this book because I have gone from being an 80-pound anorexic between the ages of 15-19, to weighing 99-112 pounds between the ages of 19-34, to weighing 162½ pounds at 34, to back down to 115 pounds at age 36. For two years, (34-36), I struggled with my weight to get back to a normal size again.

Most of my life I weighed between 99-112 pounds. Everything was great but I had anorexic tendencies. I only ate dinner, which meant that I starved my body all day long. I also exercised every day for 1½ hours to maintain my weight.

One day I noticed that I had acquired a lisp. As the days progressed, the lisp got worse until I went to a doctor. The doctor prescribed me pills and my lisp went away, but I started gaining four pounds a day. I thought my scale was broken, but then I couldn't fit into my pants. I didn't know why I was gaining so much weight, so I started exercising four hours a day just to maintain my weight.

Finally, I went back to my doctor and she took me off the pills for my lisp and said that the pills were probably the cause of my weight gain. Immediately after, I started losing weight again, but I had a long way to go because I had gone from 99 pounds to 162½ pounds. I almost doubled my size, so I had a hard time trying to lose all that weight again. It took two years. I tried every diet pill on the market and none of them really worked. Slowly, with exercise and moderate eating, I lost the weight again. It sounds so fairytale but I struggled with my weight all my life and I am still struggling.

Why I Became Anorexic

What caused me to become anorexic at age 15? When I was born, I weighed 9 pounds. I didn't want to come out of my mother's stomach. I was one month late. As I grew older, I was an average size kid—not fat and not too skinny.

At age 14, I was 5 feet 4 inches tall and weighed about 120 pounds. I wanted to be a model, so I had professional pictures taken of myself. Then my father took me to New York and we went to a few of the modeling agencies. One agency told me I was too fat, but that if I lost weight I should come back and see them again. From that time on, something triggered in my mind. I was determined to get skinny. I remember what I ate that day: lobster without the butter sauce, and I only ate a few bites of it. From that day on, I began only eating dinners and I counted every bite of food I took in. I remember going to my favorite Italian restaurant and ordering fettuccine alfredo; I ate ten noodles and I left the rest.

I began exercising at 5 a.m. every morning for 1½ hours. As I was losing weight, everyone told me how great I looked, so that stuck in my head to continue losing weight. I even got my first boyfriend at age 15 while I was getting skinny. The problem with my diet was that I got carried away and lost too much weight. I went from 120 pounds to 80 pounds in just a few months. I never threw up or took pills to go to the bathroom. I just exercised every day and ate very little.

I felt hungry all the time and all I could think about was food. I was weak. I remember lying down a lot and suffering of hunger. When I reached 80 pounds, my parents took me to a psychiatrist. The doctor said to my parents that the only way to handle a case like mine was to threaten to take things away from the anorexic. By now I was about 16 and my parents had bought me a new car, which I loved and washed every day. The psychiatrist told my parents to take the car away from me if I didn't eat. My parents didn't agree with the doctor, so we never went back to him. My parents thought that they could get me to eat without anyone's help.

I didn't stay 80 pounds for very long. It was a long, hard battle. I was weighed every night. I promised my parents that I would gain some weight as long as they didn't make me see a psychiatrist or take away my car. It took me about a year to reach 99 pounds again. At that weight, my parents and I felt satisfied.

It wasn't about control with me that made me skinny. I also didn't think I looked fat. I knew that I looked too skinny but I was afraid to get fat.

I also acquired strange habits like smelling or touching food with my fingers to satisfy my hunger rather than eating it. Another bad habit I had was that when I weighed too much, I would stay up all night and try to urinate a lot because I thought that if I went to the bathroom, I would weigh less.

Why My Parents Put Me in a Clinic

When I was 22, I graduated McGill University and then I moved to Florida with my mother. I had a lot of time on my hands before I began to work. I joined a health club with a friend of mine and I worked out all day long, every day. I also only ate one meal a day—dinner. Then I would go to sleep. That was my daily routine for a few months. I woke up, went to the gym, exercised before my friend showed up, then exercised with my friend, exercised after my friend left, went home to eat dinner, and then went to bed. My parents began to worry about me.

I weighed between 99-105 pounds, but all I did was work out, and if I missed a day I would jog around the golf course for a few hours. I got carried away again with my body, so my parents put me in an eating disorder clinic. I was there for one month, and guess what? They fed me three meals a day and no there was no exercise. I went into the clinic weighing 105 pounds and I left weighing 93 pounds. During my stay, I actually lost weight by eating three normal meals a day instead of working out all day long and only eating dinner. When the doctors saw that I lost so much weight at the clinic, they had to feed me Ensure milkshakes in between my meals so that I wouldn't lose any more weight.

When I got home, all the progress I had made at the clinic by eating three meals a day was lost. I started exercising every day, but only for 1½ hours, and I only ate dinner again. The reason I only ate dinner was because in my mind if I ate three meals a day I would get fat because my meals were not weighed out properly like they were in the clinic. It was easy to lose weight in the clinic because if I was very hungry one day, all I could eat was what was on my tray and nothing more. At home, my meals were not portioned out, so I could overeat by mistake and gain weight. The only way I saw myself staying slim alone was to limit myself to eating one meal a day.

A new problem arose because of my only eating dinner.

Around the age of 26, I started getting up in the middle of the night and eating. That was awful because I would wake up the next morning a couple of pounds heavier.

As a result, my parents put me back in a clinic. Once again, they regulated my eating habits and I left there weighing a few pounds less than I entered. I tried to eat three meals a day when I got home, but I got scared again, so I only ate dinners. I also continued to wake up in the middle of the night to eat in my sleep.

At age 27, I got tired of exercising every day for 1½ hours, so I only exercised once in a while. My weight went up a few pounds to 105-112, but I was still skinny so I didn't mind weighing more.

When I was 30 years old, I started taking laxatives occasionally. That was not a good idea because the body gets accustomed to eliminating with a laxative and you become immune to the laxative, and then you can't go to the bathroom with or without it. As soon as I would get immune to one laxative, I would try a different brand. I remember getting really sick from taking too many laxatives. I had the worst stomach cramps, which lasted all night long. I was so scared that if the cramps didn't go away by the morning I would have to go the hospital.

How I Gained 62½ Pounds

At age 33, I started to lisp a little. A few days later my lisp was really bad, so I went to a doctor to see what was wrong with me. The doctor prescribed me pills that made my lisp better, but I started gaining so much weight. By the time I reached 162½ pounds, my doctor took me off the pills; she thought the pills were the reason for my weight gain. She was right, but by this time I had gained 62½ pounds. It all happened so fast that I didn't really realize how fat I'd gotten. It took me two years to go down to about 115 pounds.

At age 34, I put myself on a waiting list to an outpatient eating disorder clinic. It was a two-year wait. By age 34, my weight had gone down from 162½ pounds to 130 pounds. I don't even know how I did it, but I was constantly watching my weight and exercising. I bought every diet pill on the market, even prescription ones, but none of them really worked. It was much harder to lose weight this time than when I was 15. One of the reasons was that I still ate in the middle of the night. I would have dinner at 7 p.m. and go to bed at 11 p.m. I usually woke up after 12 a.m. to start munching in my sleep, which always made me put on a couple of extra pounds overnight.

When I told my doctor about my bad eating habits, he prescribed me sleeping pills so that I wouldn't wake up all the time in the middle of the night to eat. He said that the reason I was eating all night long was because I was starving my body all day long, so it was a way of protecting me from getting sick.

None of the sleeping pills worked. I still woke up to eat in the middle of the night. It was very disappointing because I would starve all day long and only eat a small dinner. I could have lost a lot of weight like that but I overate in the middle of the night. I think I was really sleeping while I ate in the odd hours of the night because I don't really remember everything I had eaten when I woke up the next morning. I was sleep-eating. I was lucky that I didn't gain weight but it certainly didn't help my attempt at losing weight again. At this time, I didn't really have the energy to exercise like when I was younger.

What I did was try every diet pill on the market until saw Anna Nicole Smith on a TV interview and heard how she lost over 100 pounds. She took an appetite suppressant called TrimSpa. I immediately looked up Trim Spa on my computer. I was disappointed at first because one place told me that they didn't ship to Canada where I live. Then I called a few more numbers and finally found a place that shipped to Canada. I have to admit that the TrimSpa did help me lose some weight. It didn't always work. Some days that I took it I still overate, but the days that it did work, I managed to eat very little and I lost weight. At age 35, between the TrimSpa and occasional exercise, I lost a few more pounds.

I also got a phone call from the outpatient eating disorder clinic that I had applied to a few years earlier. They said I could make an appointment and join the clinic.

This clinic involved many interviews with several doctors and a dietician. It wasn't going to be easy. There was no magical remedy from the clinic, but it was worth it to go to all my appointments if it would help me to lose weight.

Much to my disappointment, the clinic was of no help to me. My first appointment was with a social worker who just asked me many questions but gave me no advice or remedies. My next appointment was with a psychiatrist who again asked me many questions, most of which were the same ones the social worker had asked me. My third appointment was with a dietician. She asked me the same questions as the first two. She asked me what was more important to me: to eat three meals a day or to lose weight. I told her that my main goal was to lose a bit more weight. The dietician told me that if I did eat three meals a day, I may not lose any weight and I may even gain weight. Her advice to me was that I should continue to only eat at night, but if I wanted to try to eat in the day I should do it when I was out of town. I had told her my job involved going out of town at least twice a month for five days each time, and since there was no extra food in the hotel room, it was safe to start eating three meals a day and just sleep when I get to the hotel room at night.

I met all three counselors and none of them gave me the least bit of help whatsoever. I was completely shocked because I had waited two years just to get an appointment with this clinic and I had already managed to lose 40 pounds (of the 47½ pounds that I needed to lose) all by myself.

My next step was to continue to slowly lose weight the same way I had done before. I bought a natural sleep aid called melatonin. Instead of buying diet pills, which didn't really work that well, I tried a different approach (similar to my doctor's approach) but this didn't involve a prescription and was natural. The melatonin helped me wake up less often overnight so I ate a bit less in my sleep, which was a start.

Then I tried taking laxatives once in a while. My doctor told me that Dulcolax was the most effective one. I took three Dulcolaxes whenever I noticed my weight rising. It brought my weight down a couple of pounds each time, which was great, but after a couple of days it went right back up again.

I felt like I was all alone in my battle against anorexia. Actually I wasn't because my mother was helping me all the way through. She was very patient with me and continued to give me advice on how to get slimmer again. She told me that I should eat during the day and exercise. Her advice was the best I could get because my body was starving for food and just stored anything I gave it to eat since I didn't consume anything all day long.

My mother only kept healthy foods for me to eat like salads and fruit, and no junk food. That helped me not gain weight. The only thing I couldn't do was eat during the day. I had a mental block thinking that I would gain weight if I ate all day long as well as all night long. I didn't believe that if I ate during the day I would stop eating at night.

As I said before, my new job required that I travel a lot, which was lucky for me because there was no food in the hotel room for me to eat in my sleep. At home, I just went into the refrigerator, freezer, or pantry all night long, which made me stay fat. As a result of my traveling, my weight went down to 120 pounds, which was not too far from my goal weight of 115 pounds. The only problem was that when I came home again for a couple of days, I gained a few pounds again until I traveled and lost only what I had gained from being home. My weight at this time was 120-125 pounds. When I traveled, I was 120. When I came home, I was 125.

At this point I tried diet pills again, but natural ones. The first thing I tried didn't work, but I was told that I'd need to buy a few different pills together and that should work, so I tried that. Guess what? Instead of weighing 125 pounds when I came home, I went down to 120 pounds at home. I still only ate dinner but the pills burned some of my fat from the food I ate in my sleep. Now these pills don't have any effect anymore. They worked for a couple of weeks but not now.

I never went back to the hospital that was supposed to help me eat three meals a day because they really couldn't do anything for me. They also couldn't guarantee that I would lose weight; they'd said I may even gain weight, which is an anorexic's nightmare.

A trick that I tried was to suck on sugar-free candies whenever I got hungry, but it only helped me when I was out of town because there was nothing to eat in the hotel room. When I was home, regardless of how many candies I ate while I was awake, I still ate in the middle of the night, so it was twice as bad because I ate the candies and food from the kitchen in my sleep.

Starting to Eat Three Meals a Day

I noticed a coorelation between what I ate and how much I would weigh the next day. Whenever I ate bread or crackers I gained weight the next day, but if I ate things like fish, meat, chicken, salads, or fruits, I would either stay the same weight or lose weight. I think the worst thing to eat is bread. I also noticed that when I got my monthly menstrual cycle, I gained about two pounds, so I ended up exercising for the five days that I had my menstruation.

Once I reached 120 pounds, the last five pounds were extremely difficult to lose.

I do live infomercials for a living out of town in large department stores. I really enjoy my job. Just today a lady gave me a big hug and a kiss and told me that she wants to take me home to show her how to use the houseware products that I sell. That happens to me a lot. Another person in the audience thought I was Sarah Michelle Gellar. Another time, a guy screamed out during the infomercial, "Will you marry me? I am a lawyer." Many times people clap for me or tell me how pretty I am or how much they like me. I have only been doing this job for a year. When I lost my voice, I was working in my mother's gambling bar so my voice wasn't as important to me. Now I rely on my voice all the time to make a living, so I am upset about my voice not being perfect.

At this time, because it took so long to lose the last five pounds to reach my goal weight of 115 pounds, I was desperate and I thought I should take advantage of my traveling time when I stayed in hotels. I was scared and apprehensive at first, but my mother helped me.

Slowly I began to eat three meals a day, and when I got back to the hotel I didn't eat because there was no fridge or pantry. My meals were portioned out since I ate in restaurants, which limited my overeating.

The first day, I only ate a fruit cup for breakfast, a sandwich for lunch, and some fish for dinner. It didn't take long before I lost one pound from 120 to 119. I stuck to my diet of forcing myself to eat three meals a day and I lost all the weight I wanted. I am now115 pounds. I eat three times a day and I exercise whenever I can.

It seems pretty easy to maintain my weight and not gain it back because as soon as I got to 116½ pounds, I didn't really want to eat because I was so happy being skinny again. I still made sure that I ate three meals a day and exercised at least twice a week. I never binge like I did when I only ate once a day because I didn't starve my body all day and wasn't hungry.

Eating three meals a day is not an easy thing to do for an anorexic. In the beginning, I counted every mouthful I ate and I remember chewing very slowly. It took me twice as long to eat as it did my mother. My mother was very supportive in my battle against anorexia. She is very skinny and so is my father. My mother told me years ago that if I ate three meals a day I wouldn't be so hungry at dinner or eat in the middle of the night anymore. I realize now that she was right. Also, the fact that I travel a lot helps me not binge or eat in my sleep either.

Now I eat more with my three meals than I did with my one meal and sleep-eating, and I lost the last five pounds in just a few days. I eat more now than I ever remember eating and I am staying 115 pounds. I haven't had three meals a day since I was 14 years old because I have been anorexic since I was 15.

At 115 pounds, everything is fun to do. For example, I look forward to going to work because my body looks good.

I remember hating to get out of bed when I was heavier. Now I love everything and I am happy when I put on my clothes and look in the mirror. I even bought a couple of tank tops that I wear now but couldn't put on when I was 162½ pounds.

How I Tricked My Family and Stayed Under 99 Pounds

When I look back at my anorexic days, I can't believe I am still alive. I remember when I moved from Montreal and I weighed 99 pounds or a little less, and my brother would visit my mother and me. He would weigh me every day to make sure I wasn't less than 99 pounds. I was so scared that I would drink three large bottles of water right before I got weighed so it put a few extra pounds of weight on me. That was when I was about 21 years old. Again, my father threatened to take away my Mazda RX7 if I was lighter than 99 pounds. I learned that water trick from a friend I met in the eating disorder clinic. Drinking water before I got weighed temporarily raised my weight, and then a few hours later I'd urinate it out and be back to being skinny again.

I don't know how I did it. I was studying pre-med in Florida at Barry University. While my brother was visiting, I had to drink three large bottles of water while I was studying because he would weigh me after school. I had to drink the water in just a few minutes, so I got the worst headaches. After that I couldn't really study but I was smart and I managed to get away with studying less. Besides, my brother only visited for a couple of weeks just a few times a year. I loved my brother and my parents and I knew they were only trying to make sure I didn't get sick or anything.

When I weighed 99 pounds, I rarely drank anything because I thought that I would rather eat a grapefruit than drink grapefruit juice. Drinking seemed to put weight on me and I didn't think I was getting any pleasure or satisfaction out of drinking. It took longer to eat a fruit than to drink it and I thought there were more calories in a drink than in one fruit.

My thoughts were consumed all the time with what I would eat for dinner. If I had a party to go to the following day, I would not eat dinner the night before so that I looked normal eating with everyone else at the party.

If I didn't know a day in advance that I had to go out with

a friend for breakfast or lunch, then I had to lie about not being able to join them. I remember going with my cousin, her husband, her kids, and my aunt and uncle for lunch and to the park. I made up an excuse that I had a meeting for work and that I couldn't make it for lunch but I could see them after at the park if they wanted. That is a typical example of what I did all the time when it came to eating breakfast or lunch with friends or family members. I just called them up on my cell phone to ask when they were going to the park and completely avoided the food topic. I think everyone really knew that I was lying about a meeting just to avoid eating with them but nobody ever said anything. I am not the type of person to lie about anything, but my anorexia left me with no choice very often.

I ate very slowly. I chewed every mouthful very slowly. I wanted my food to last as long as possible because I enjoyed eating my dinner very much. If I eat a lot of animal protein, I don't wake up as much in the middle of the night to eat more food.When I eat pasta or bread, I eat again and again and again all night long.

My anorexic symptoms were not very pleasant to live with. I remember always being cold. My hands and feet felt cold and my body was constantly shivering. I never liked to take pictures of myself. I knew I was too skinny but I was afraid to get fat, so I just stayed too skinny. I looked so ugly when I was under 103 pounds. I was a very cute baby. I was an ugly pre-teen and teen until I gained some weight and was at least 103 pounds. Now, at 37 and 115 pounds, I never looked better.

I am very lucky to have nice parents like I do because I certainly wasn't an easy child to bring up. I never ate at the same time as the family. I would wait until I was so hungry that I just couldn't wait any more to eat.

When I was in school studying pre-med and I was just under 99 pounds, I starved my body all day long until I got home at 2 a.m. Often I was uncomfortable with my friends because they would eat and I would just watch or accompany them but not eat with them. As a result, I didn't eat the night before so I could eat with my friends in the cafeteria the next day. I only did that if I was sure we would plan a get-together. If it wasn't planned a day before, I sat uncomfortably watching my friends watch me not eat.

I am not a closet eater or a binger. Actually, I prefer to eat in front of people for some reason. I think it's because I want them to think I am normal and that I do eat.

I weigh myself ten times a day: after every meal or every drink I take, after I go to the washroom, when I wake up, and when I go to sleep. Now I travel a lot but I always pack my scale with me.

When I was exercising every day and in school, I couldn't exercise before school because my classes started at 8 a.m. I felt fat every morning until my break from school, when I'd run to my health club to exercise.

After exercising I felt great, so I wasn't always miserable—just when I was fat, according to my standards. When I was skinny, I was the happiest person in the world. I even used to wear fat or skinny clothes. On days that I was fat I wore black, and on days that I was skinny I wore white.

I also had crazy fetishes when I was anorexic. I lived in Florida for a few years, so on the weekends I often ran to the beach to sit in the sun because I wanted to sweat away my fat. Also, I often went to the washroom to urinate because I thought it would help me lose more weight.

I didn't like to go out after I ate my dinner because I always felt full and uncomfortable, so I tried to do everything I had to do before I ate dinner.

I am not saying that I am completely cured of all my habits and anorexia, but I do eat three meals a day now. I do go out after I eat and walk around on a full stomach but I am not really comfortable being too full unless I am at home and ready to go to bed. I try to only eat small portions and not let myself get too full during the day.

I remember sometimes on days when I ate a lot I was afraid to weigh myself, so what I did was feel my cheekbones to see if they were there, and also I would try on my pants to see if they were too tight. If I felt cheekbones and my pants were not too tight, I would weigh myself, but if I couldn't feel my cheekbones and my pants were too tight, I wouldn't weigh myself and I would try not to eat that day. Now I weigh myself every day no matter what. I am not scared anymore because I don't overeat.

What Type of Foods Keep the Weight Off

I think that weighing your food is a good way to stay thin. For example, I would rather eat popcorn or licorice over ice cream. Also, I would rather eat fish over steak. You have to be careful when you do this because people tend to think that since the food weighs less, they can eat more of it, which is not good since it defeats the whole purpose.

The same thing goes for diet foods. They may have fewer calories but you can't eat more of it or it can be just as bad as eating regular fattening foods. A good example of this is rice cakes. They weigh very little and they have only a few calories, so it's common for people to eat more of them, which can be just as bad as eating bread or crackers.

Drinking water is much better for you than anything else because it has no calories and helps in your elimination process.

Another thing that helped me lose weight when I wasn't in a hotel was to have less food in the house so you don't get carried away with testing a whole bunch of different things. If I didn't eat in a restaurant, I would buy something to take out and have an empty refrigerator and pantry. That way the food is already portioned out for you, and if you get hungry there is nothing to eat or drink but water.

When I first became anorexic about 22 years ago, people didn't really know what it was. I didn't know what it was either. I never said, "Oh, I would like to be anorexic now." I just ate very little, exercised excessively, and lost a lot of weight in a short period of time. I don't think anyone wants to be anorexic. A lot of anorexics die or get sick. It is definitely not something to be proud of, especially since anorexics tend to get too skinny so they are not very pretty.

I think it would have been hard for me to get married when I was anorexic because I only ate once a day and any husband would think that was crazy. Plus he wouldn't have enjoyed being with me since there is a famous expression: the key to a man's heart is through his stomach. Many men love to eat and it wouldn't be fair to me or him if he ate alone or I watched him eat. Also, I wouldn't want to have kids unless they were adopted because I would be afraid to gain weight during my pregnancy. Some anorexics can't get pregnant even if they want to because many don't get their monthly menstruation. When I was younger I lost my period for a year so. I had to go to the doctor and he prescribed me something called Provera. That helped me get my monthly menstruation back and now I am fine, so I was lucky.

I eat more of a variety of foods now compared to when I was anorexic. I used to eat the same foods for weeks at a time because I got used to the portions. For example, I remember eating this for dinner: one can of tuna, one baked potato, two apples and popcorn. I knew when I ate this portion that I didn't gain weight, so it was easy and safe for me.

Now I eat different foods all the time. I don't like to eat home-cooked meals because I tend to overeat, and I am in hotels most of the time anyway. I enjoy eating in restaurants and taking food out.

I think that elimination is very important to maintain a healthy weight. It's good to eat fruits, vegetables and fiber. I am not saying that I have a Ph.D. in healthy bodies but I did go through a lot in my life and I have experienced quite a bit more on this subject matter than most people. I did study pre-med and I got accepted into medical school and studied as a nurse's aide, so I do have some knowledge behind me.

When I was about 21, I had a boyfriend who was very, very skinny. I am not sure if he had anorexia or not but we never went out to eat together. He just liked to stay up late and talk. He looked skinnier than me and I was only 99 pounds. When I saw him six years later, he had doubled in size. He wasn't too fat but he wasn't considered too skinny anymore. He also ate in front of me a lot. It seems that you can get over anorexia, but most people when they do end up gaining a lot of weight.

I grew up in one of the richest areas in Canada. We lived in a mansion with five floors, six Jacuzzis, a pool, and two saunas. My bedroom overlooked the pool. I liked to swim as often as possible. It was a long, kidney-shaped pool where I did laps to keep in shape. I also had a rowing machine in my bedroom that was the same as the ones in the gym. If I ate a little too much, I would row it off. It was amazing. I've always had some kind of exercise equipment in my room because as an anorexic I don't think I could live without it.

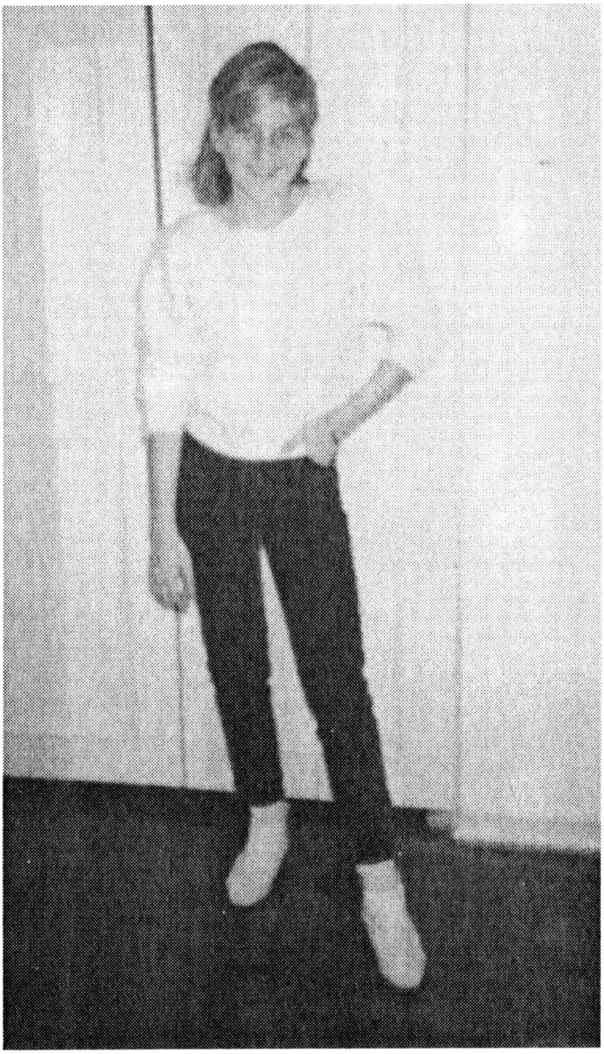

Me at age 15, 70 to 80 pounds.

*Me now, age 38,
115 pounds.*

My father.

My mother.

The house where I grew up.

How Pills Made Me Gain 62½ Pounds

I grew up relatively slim, but at age 15 I gained a few extra pounds. From 15 to 21 I weighed between 80-99 pounds. From 21 to 34 I weighed 99-112 pounds. At 34, I lost my voice and my doctor gave me a combination of several pills to get my voice back, but it made me gain 62½ pounds. Between 34 and 36 I went down from 162½ pounds to 115 pounds, which is what I weigh now. For most of my life, from 15 to 34, I was anorexic. Most anorexics don't ever recover, but I feel like I have somewhat. I had relatively no help except for my family. I don't wish this disease on anyone or any family.

When I started getting fat, I didn't believe it. I thought my scale was broken, so I bought a new scale, but that also showed I was gaining weight.

I know it was the pills that caused my weight gain but I don't think pills alone can make you heavier. The pills cause you to have an increase in appetite, which causes you to eat more and therefore gain weight. I was eating three ice cream bars a day as a snack. I ate constantly and that's what made me fat.

It was a terrible feeling gaining weight. My pants were too tight and I had to buy new jeans because all my clothes were too small.

I tried going to several doctors to get diet pills by prescription, which I thought would work for sure. I found a nice, cute doctor who felt bad for me when I told him my story. He gave me a prescription for an appetite suppressant, which cost a few hundred dollars but didn't work. Since I was stuck with all those pills, I figured maybe if I waited a couple of weeks and then tried them again they may work for a day or so, but they didn't.

I have never been fat my whole life. I looked like a completely different person. My face got fat and I had a mean look in my eye that was no fault of mine since I couldn't control it; I was bloated and my eyes were just permanently mean-looking.

When I noticed I was getting fat, I immediately bought an aerobicycle. I started exercising every day for four hours a day. The pills gave me a lot of energy so I even worked out at 3 a.m.. I gained four pounds a day unless I exercised four hours or more each day.

Tricks That Help Me Keep the Weight Off

One of the things that kept me going while I was losing the weight was that if I starved myself a few times a week and lost a bit of weight, then I could eat almost anything I wanted when I got back to my goal weight and never gain weight again. It was worth it because I suffered a few days a week but I knew that once I got skinny again, I could practically eat anything I wanted. I don't really know how I lost all that weight again but it wasn't easy, and I hope I don't have that happen to me ever again.

Now I eat my regular meals but I stop eating before I finish everything on my plate. I like to have a little bit of food left over. It requires a bit of discipline because I would like to finish everything on my plate or even try for seconds, but I don't. My entire life I've had success by leaving some food on my plate and I will try to always do that.

Another thing I noticed about maintaining my goal weight is I do get to eat just about anything I want and I don't gain weight, whereas if I had to lose weight I had to suffer by eating much less and by exercising more.

Something that I do when I get thirsty or hungry after I eat my meal is chew sugar-free gum. It does seem to tide me over until I eat again.

I think hunger feelings don't last very long, and if you can beat them you may not get hungry again until a couple of hours later. Ways that I beat hunger is by chewing sugar-free gum or taking a sip of a diet soft drink or water. I like sugar-free products but I hear that they are unhealthy for you. I think many things are unhealthy for you, so I still eat sugar-free things because they do help me stay slim.

Something new that I heard was to drink green tea every day for a month and you are supposed to lose eight pounds after the first month.

There are so many things you hear in the news that you don't know whether or not to believe. It just so happens that I find when I eat a lot during the day, I don't tend to drink very much. Also, days when I drink a lot I don't seem to eat much. Some days I am hungrier and I don't drink, whereas other days when I am thirstier I don't eat. It seems to coincide with the belief that it is not good to eat and drink at the same meal. They say you should wait until a couple of hours after eating to drink.

I don't like to eat very late at night because I find I end up eating a lot more than if I eat dinner earlier. If I buy something to eat and I end up eating very late, I eat faster and I end up eating something else too. Now as soon as I get hungry, I eat.

I don't exercise as much as I did when I was anorexic and I don't really enjoy it either. What I do to make it less of a pain is watch my favorite program, *Buffy the Vampire Slayer*, or listen to the radio while I exercise, which makes it a lot more enjoyable.

I think exercise is important for everyone to do, even if they don't need to lose weight, because it's healthy for your heart and bones. I know someone who has been very skinny her whole life and never exercised. Now that she's older, her doctor told her to exercise because her heart is weak and she needs a pacemaker. If she exercised now and then when she was younger, she wouldn't need a pacemaker.

This may sound crazy, but in the past couple of years I've developed a new bad phobia about gaining weight. I only took a shower or a bath when I was having a fat day because I thought that if I got wet, the open pores in my skin would absorb the water and make me heavier than I already was. The day was already bad, so it couldn't get much worse. On my skinny days, I didn't want to get heavier just because I needed to take a shower, so I waited.

I don't like to cook foods because it makes me hungry even when I started out not being hungry. That's why I only eat out or I buy take-out foods. I have a little trick that I play on myself. It takes about one minute or two to eat a snack or a few minutes to eat an entire meal, so I just ask myself: "Is it worth it to eat something now, because it will only last me a few minutes and I may get a couple of pounds heavier." What I do is pretend that I ate, the few minutes are up but I really don't eat and I end up staying the same weight instead of indulging in food that only lasts a few minutes but can add a few extra pounds too.

I never really had any therapy for my anorexia. I've tried several times but it never worked out. I had to go through all this by myself with the help of my mother, my father, and my brothers. I don't really think there is any magical therapy to cure something like this. I am very strong-willed and that must contribute to my surviving this disease.

When I gained the 62½ pounds, I thought I would never be able to get back to my comfortable weight again, but I did and I think it's a miracle. It took a long time but I did it. Whenever people see me since I was fat, they can't believe how I lost all that weight.

One of my mother's friends always says to me, "You look so great! I can't believe you lost all that weight!"

It's really a nice feeling to hear people telling me how great I look now. I just hope nothing like that ever happens again because I don't know if I could go through such a dramatic weight loss three times in my life. I don't think it's healthy to gain and lose so much weight so many times.

Now whenever I eat too much, my stomach gets really sore so I can't eat anything else. It really stops me from eating any more for that meal. I don't remember that ever happening to me before, but my body has really changed and naturally keeps me from gaining weight.

I just finished exercising on my aerobicycle. I was on for an hour because today I weighed 117 pounds instead of 115 and I lost the two pounds after only an hour of exercise. That's why for me it is important to have an exercise machine in my house. It's not only that I was 117 pounds but the fact that if I didn't keep my weight at 115, then I may be two pounds heavier the following day and so on. That's how a person can gain weight. I am on top of my weight now because I will never forget how those pills made me gain four pounds a day and I exercised four hours a day. How hard is it to exercise for an hour if it's going to keep you thin and healthy?

At 115 pounds, I am so happy. I am used to always being skinny, so I don't think I will really gain back much weight. There's a big difference between having to lose weight and just maintaining your weight. When I had to lose weight, I resorted to doing many things that I was against, such as taking diet pills and laxatives. As I said, they don't really work well but they probably helped a little bit. I don't take anything like that anymore. They scare me. Actually, a few weeks ago, I took a new diet pill and my heart was palpitating. I got so scared that I told my mother I took a diet pill. She was furious and threw them out right away. I lay down and got better after a few hours. Now I don't go near a diet pill or a laxative ever.

I still get hungry every now and then between meals, so I drink a few sips of black coffee or green tea and that seems to curb my appetite for a few hours. Actually, it's 4 p.m. now while I am writing this book and I am hungry, so I made some green tea and I'll feel fine until dinner.

I have so many clothes. I fit into almost everything that I had my whole life until I got fat for a couple of years. I didn't buy many clothes when I was fat because I knew I wouldn't be like that for very long.

It was so scary when I gained weight. I didn't even believe it for a while until I just couldn't fit into any of my clothes and I bought a new scale. It all happened so fast. I ate so much junk food that I blew up right away. Sweets are very bad to eat. If I eat a cookie or a chocolate bar, I try to eat fewer other foods that day. Sweets don't seem to satisfy my hunger. Once, I had three chocolate bars in one day and I was still hungry. When I weighed myself, I didn't gain any weight that day because a chocolate bar doesn't weigh that much, but the next day it stuck in my body and caused me to gain weight because I didn't burn off those extra calories and fat. The same thing happens to me with bread or cake. It's hard to burn off those calories and I end up gaining weight the next day. Fruits and vegetables weigh more than a chocolate bar or bread, so you can weigh more as soon as you eat them but you can burn off the calories easier so the next day you are slimmer. They also seem to fill me up and satisfy my hunger.

You can also gain weight by eating too much. Portions are important. I try not to take seconds and I stop eating before I get full.

Exercise is very important, even if it's just a short walk around the block. When I have my days off, I seem to gain more weight if I stay at home and don't exercise. I don't eat more but I burn off less calories if I don't go out.

It's amazing how food is such an important factor in an anorexic's life. I would love to eat junk food but I don't like the consequences of gaining weight that goes with it. Anorexics seem to have a lot of discipline staying anorexic-skinny, which means giving up a lot of pleasures in life, such as eating sweets, lazing around all day, drinking liquor in clubs or going to parties, going out with friends, and getting married and having a baby.

When I was too skinny, I couldn't even get a boyfriend because I looked so ugly. My face was full of pimples because I lacked vitamins in my diet, my hair was fuzzy, and my bones cracked every time someone hugged me.

My mother made me laugh when I told her I was writing this book. She told me that when I didn't eat, she didn't eat either because she felt uncomfortable eating alone.

My parents are very skinny. I remember when I ate dinner I ate so slowly because I wanted it to last as long as possible. It caused my father to eat slowly because he was uncomfortable watching me eat and taking a lot longer than anyone else. It's good to eat slowly because you realize you are full with less food, but I ate one noodle at a time. For example, if I ate Kraft Dinner or fettuccine alfredo, I only ate one noodle at a time. It took forever to eat my meal, but most of the time I didn't finish my plate anyway.

Now that I am 115 pounds, I try to eat my three meals a day. I enjoy eating out a lot, but for breakfast I prefer to eat at home because I don't like to eat a big breakfast. I find that eating breakfast out is too much food for me. Since I am out of town most of the time, I usually buy a banana and yogurt from a supermarket and eat something like that for breakfast instead of eating eggs, bacon, and toast or pancakes at a restaurant.

Lunch and dinner are not as difficult. I can eat a sandwich for lunch and fish or chicken for dinner. The portions in a restaurant are just fine for me.

If it wasn't for my mother, I probably would still be anorexic and only eat dinner. I work with my mother and live with her too, so we eat together all the time.

Sometimes we share a meal if it looks too big and sometimes I take half of what she ordered and she takes half of what I ordered. It's more fun and a lot safer for me to eat with someone else. Sometimes if my mother goes out and I am at home for dinner, I end up eating too much because she doesn't portion out my food for me or I don't see her portion out her own food. Yesterday my mother went out for dinner and I was at home alone. I ended up eating seconds and cooking extra food and I gained two pounds.

A major reason why I overcame anorexia was because I would wake up all night long to eat, which kept my mother awake too since I live with her. She would get really angry with me and threaten to make me move out on my own. My mother loves me and would never throw me out of the house but she really got mad when I woke up so many times in the middle of the night to eat. Actually, I told her not to let me eat in my sleep, so she had to be hard on me or I wouldn't listen because I was asleep.

I didn't like getting up in the middle of the night to eat either because I always weighed a few pounds more by the morning. It bothered my mother so much and I gained a few pounds every morning. I started eating three meals a day to satisfy my hunger during the day so that I wouldn't run around all night long eating up everything in sight in my sleep.

Life in Eating Disorder Clinics

When I first became anorexic, I didn't know what it was, but my mother knew. She said that I looked too skinny and she had to beg me to eat a pea. My mother also knew that I lacked protein because I didn't eat much of it, so when they put me in an eating disorder clinic, the clinic fed me a lot of protein and three full meals a day to give me back my strength and my mind. My mother said my mind wasn't thinking rationally.

I don't even really remember everything I did just before I went to the clinic. My mother just told me, "You won't love me now, but when you're better, you will thank me." That was when they put me in an inpatient clinic, which means I had to sleep there.

When I was in the clinic, there were a lot of others like me there, as well as bulimics, alcoholics, and even drug addicts. Since there were bulimics they had locks on the outside of all the bathrooms and the staff watched you go to the bathroom just in case someone tried to throw up. I never, ever did and never, ever will throw up.

At nighttime they had separate meetings for anorexics, bulimics, alcoholics, and drug addicts. It turned out that I had fun there. I went to all of the meetings—even the alcoholics' and drug addicts' meetings. I met my best friend Allyson there in the clinic.

I was so afraid to gain weight since I didn't exercise there and I was eating three large meals a day. I exercised in my room where nobody caught me. I did sit-ups, push-ups, jogging on the spot, stretches, etc., every day and they never caught me. They also weighed us every day but they didn't tell us how much we weighed. I didn't like that because I couldn't tell if I was gaining or losing weight. They only told me my weight when I left. I had no idea that I lost about ten pounds during my one-month stay there. If they would have told me how much I weighed every day, I think I would have been a little more cooperative. I sometimes yelled when I felt they were feeding me too much. If they would have told me I was losing weight and they had to feed me more, then of course I would have eaten more. Instead they just fed me more without telling me that I was losing so much weight.

My mother came to visit me every day. I feel bad now for my parents. I don't wish an anorexic child on anyone. My eating habits were atrocious. I rarely ate with the family. I constantly lied about eating. Often I said I ate earlier when I really hadn't had anything at all. I made all kinds of noise in the house while I was exercising in the middle of the night, which interrupted my parents' sleep. I walked around looking like a toothpick; my parents must have been embarrassed to tell their friends about me. I was always lying in bed because I felt weak and hungry. My parents constantly worried that I ate healthy, even if it wasn't a lot. They also made sure that I was a certain weight and didn't fall below that, or they would have had to put me in another hospital or clinic. This is a lifetime disease that affects the whole family, not just the anorexic.

The problem with these clinics is that I got better and ate three meals a day only during my stay there. I tried for one day to eat three meals but I gained weight because I ended up eating portions that were too big for me.

When I came back to Montreal for a few months, my parents put me in another hospital. It was completely different from the one in Florida. I was an inpatient but they didn't have locks on the outsides of the bathrooms or force you to eat three meals a day.

Instead, they had menus; I could plan what I wanted to eat each day. We filled out the menu sheet the day before and we were fed what we ordered. They didn't force me to eat everything on my plate but they did have a minimum amount that we had to eat. The reason that my parents put me back in another hospital was that I had a chemical imbalance in my brain, so the doctors had to put me on pills. I think the chemical imbalance was caused by my anorexia. I hardly ate, and when I did it wasn't until dinnertime. Again, by the time I left the hospital after one month, I'd lost a few pounds.

When we went back to Florida, I didn't want to take the pills that the doctor gave me, so I ended up back in another inpatient clinic a few years later. The first clinic fixed me with food, the second clinic fixed me with pills, and this clinic fixed me with pills too. There were no menus and the food wasn't so great, but they didn't force us to eat all of the food on our plates either. However, they did force us to take our pills every day at the same time.

This place made us take a shower and wash our hair every day. I remember the air conditioning was so cold that I froze, especially the first couple of days when we could only wear a hospital gown, which was not very long and not very warm.

There wasn't much to do in this place. Most of the time we could watch television or read magazines. I think my mother visited me every day or almost every day.

After the last clinic, I took the pills regularly and didn't miss a day. I didn't want to end up going to another hospital again. I don't really mind these hospitals or clinics but I now realize how important it is to take my pills for my chemical imbalance.

I went to one more hospital for my anorexia but this was just as an outpatient. There was a two-year waiting list. I put myself on the list after I gained 62½ pounds from the pills I was given for my voice. By the time I was accepted into the hospital, I lost most of the weight. I talked about this hospital earlier on in the book and how they helped me the least of all the hospitals and clinics I went to.

What did I learn from all of this? That I need to take my pills for my chemical imbalance all the time for the rest of my life and that I need to eat three meals a day. If I don't do these things, I get physically and mentally sick.

When I was anorexic, my mother told me that I was so obsessed with exercising that she asked the spa to pretend the electricity went out to get me off the Stairmaster. My mother spoke to my doctors every day about my progress. She said the doctors told her I was progressing very well. Usually my stays in the hospitals or clinics were for about one month. The first clinic I went to was scary to me, and after one month I wanted to leave because my friend I'd met there had left already. I bribed the chief of staff with crystals that my mother gave me. They represented all positive energy like good health, love, and happiness, and I gave them to the doctor. The next day she let me go back home with my mother to Turnberry

Isle, where we lived. But I was also physically and mentally ready to go by then.

It is very dangerous to live as an anorexic. What are some of the things that I suffer permanently from being anorexic?

1. I got a chemical imbalance in my brain, and as a result I must take pills for the rest of my life.
2. I lost my voice for a year because I tried taking fewer pills for my chemical imbalance since I felt the pills made me tired all the time. I thought if I took fewer pills I would still be okay but perhaps not as tired. As a result, I began to lisp. Then I lost my voice, so the doctors had to raise my pills back to the original dosage again.
3. The doctors gave me new pills to get my voice back, on top of the pills that I was already taking. That's what caused me to gain 62½ pounds.
4. I never got married because I was more comfortable living with my mother and I felt safer too.
5. I never had kids because I never got married and I am afraid to gain weight.
6. I suffer at my job because I do live infomercials, so my voice has to be perfect but it isn't, and I probably miss out on some business.

Life at 115 Pounds

I went to my first party last night since I overcame anorexia. It was completely different for me. I didn't prepare by exercising and starving myself a day earlier. I ate a normal meal with everyone, which was my third meal of the day.

I think my body has adjusted to not exercising much and eating three times a day. I am always 115 pounds and I eat a lot. I don't really know if 115 pounds is a good weight for me or not. I am only 5' 4" tall. I don't look that skinny anymore. It's hard to get used to because I weighed about 10-15 pounds less most of my life.

I feel a lot better when I eat three meals a day compared to only eating dinner. I don't feel full or anything, but rather content. I just finished eating dinner. I had two salmon patties and a salad. That was enough to satisfy me. When dinner was my only meal, I'd eat two salmon patties, salad, corn, tuna, yogurt, a chocolate bar and Diet Coke. I ate all of that in half the time it takes me to eat my dinner now. It's as though I ate all three meals in one meal.

I used to feel light-headed during the day, as though I was pushing my body to the point of starvation all the time. I felt like my mind wasn't working properly and everything was difficult to do. I was weak and I didn't go out much because I had little or no energy to do things. I spent a lot of time in bed. I was weak and hungry.

Now I choose my foods properly and I try to eat healthy things. I take my time eating. I also prefer to eat in front of people. It's exactly the opposite as before. I don't feel light-headed anymore and I am calmer inside and out.

I don't know how I did it. If it was only 4 p.m. and I got hungry, I just didn't eat. Instead, I would lie down and try to sleep it off. I wouldn't allow myself to eat before 7 p.m. Then I ate in my sleep. In the morning, I was so full and I gained weight too. As a result, I had to take laxatives to help me go to the bathroom. I also had to exercise to help me get rid of the extra weight I put on from eating uncontrollably at night.

I think it's harder to lose weight when you get older.

When I was 15, it was easy to eat less. I went from about 120 pounds to 80 pounds in just a few months. I didn't throw up, take laxatives, or even exercise in the beginning.

The older I got, the worse and more complicated my symptoms of anorexia became. The only thing I never did was throw up. That's bulimia, and I was anorexic.

When I gained the 62½ pounds, I gained it really fast but it took a couple of years to lose it again. If I didn't gain that weight, I probably would still be anorexic. I was anorexic for 19 years. I gave up a major part of my life living with this disease. If I continued to live as an anorexic, I am sure I would have run into more problems or even die.

If I didn't eat three meals a day, I wouldn't be only 115 pounds now. I would be heavier. I think I have cured myself and I hope nothing happens to me when I get older as a result of all the pain and suffering I put my body through during my anorexic days. I am putting anorexia aside for now so I can get on with my life and live happily ever after.

The Neurologist

I went to see a neurologist today because my speech is not perfect yet. He was very nice with me. He said that it is possible that the pills I take for my chemical imbalance cause my voice to be imperfect. He gave me a few options: to go off all pills completely, or to take atypical pills that don't have any side effects.

He also sent me for blood tests and a 24-hour urine sample to test if I have too much copper in my system. If that's the case, all I have to do is reduce my copper intake and my voice could get better.

As a final test, he gave me a prescription for a pill that

works on the body immediately. He said that if the pill doesn't work right away, we can rule out that problem. Well, it didn't work.

I am going for my blood test and 24-hour urine sample tomorrow and I hope I can get my voice to work perfectly again.

This neurologist was much better than the one I went to a few years ago. The other neurologist gave me a CT scan on my brain and said there was nothing wrong with me. I asked how he could tell me that there was nothing wrong with me when I couldn't talk properly.

This new doctor said that he can hear that my voice is a little off-key and he is taking steps to get my voice back 100%.

My own doctor is an absolute doll. He even calls me on weekends because I complain about my voice. He made my voice much better with a new pill. It's still not perfect, but it's much better.

My mother heard something that really got through to me: you have to realize that you're enough. That's self-confidence. That is something we have to realize in life. Focus on doing positive things that add to your life instead of destroying your life.

Interview with My Father

1. How and when could you tell that I'd gotten so skinny?

Anne, you wore loose clothes, so I didn't notice right away. Then when I weighed you you were 69 pounds, so I had to bring you to the hospital.

(I thought my lowest weight was 80 pounds but my father says I was 69 pounds.)

2. Did it affect your eating habits?

It did not affect my eating habits. I had two kids;

> one was very overweight and the other was very underweight. So I had to try to set an example for both of them. I told Anne to eat some healthy foods, and I told Bruce that if he lost weight I'd offer him what he wanted most in the world, and he said he wanted a Ferrari. I also went and jogged with Bruce every day, hoping that would help him lose weight.
>
> For Anne, who was much more serious, I brought her to a psychiatrist for help.

We didn't listen to the psychiatrist by returning and force-feeding me in his office and taking away all my privileges. Instead, my father and I worked together endless hours every day to try to bring up my weight. My father weighed me every day for at least a year, and every time I gained a bit of weight, it bothered me but it pleased my father tremendously. Sometimes I tricked my father by changing the scale's calibration, wearing heavy clothing, or putting things in my pockets.

The funniest and craziest thing I did was when my parents put me in a hospital, I remember escaping and going right back to the gym to finish my workout. My parents had to come back and take me back to the hospital, which was 50 miles away.

Things to Think About If You Want Help with Anorexia

If you are anorexic and want to get back to eating normally again, there are several things you have to do:

1. First of all, you have to want to cure yourself and realize that you are sick. You can't live as an anorexic and expect not to suffer from illnesses such as brain disorders, heart troubles, or any sickness that results when you don't feed your body and mind properly. It may not

manifest itself right away but it can happen in a few years from now. It's very dangerous not to feed your body properly. We eat to live, so if you don't eat, how can you expect to live? For some people, something bad has to happen to them before they think they need to overcome anorexia.

2. Second, you have to want to look pretty or handsome. Anorexics look sick and ugly. The problem with anorexia is that they can't tell how skinny they look. In fact, they think they look fat. Not only is an anorexic too skinny-looking, but her hair looks bad, her skin looks ugly, her nails are brittle, etc. These are things that people spend countless dollars on every day to look better. When the body lacks vitamins, which you get from food, you can't look good. Your hair gets frizzy, your skin gets full of pimples, and your bones stick out.

3. You may want to get help either from a hospital or clinic or from a friend or family member. An anorexic needs help. It's very difficult to cure yourself on your own.

A clinic or hospital can give you a step in the right direction. They can show you that by eating three meals a day, you may not gain weight. It's a stable environment and there are doctors available 24 hours a day in case something goes wrong. If you have anorexia for many years, something has to happen to your mental or physical health. You can't live in a hospital or clinic forever but they can guide you to feeding yourself properly.

A friend or family member can help you out at home. It

should be someone you trust and preferably someone who is relatively thin too so that you won't think they will make you fat. The last thing an anorexic wants to become is fat. You can eat exactly what that friend or family member eats. That may help guide you in a more realistic way compared to starving yourself all day long.

4. You have to make a plan. Perhaps you can see a dietician who can give you a day-by-day menu to follow and show you correct portion sizes. Try to prepare in advance what you are going to eat for the day. That way, you won't go under or over the amount

If you exercise every day, plan to exercise every second day. Your body will feel less beat up and tired or sore. Don't give up exercising, because it is healthy for you. Just try it less often or for not as long.

5. Start right now. The longer you wait, the worse your anorexia becomes and the more harm you do to your body. Often anorexics are very rigid. Use this to your advantage. Make a schedule of things you will eat and do and stick to it.

Try one or all of these steps and see if they can help you overcome anorexia like they did for me. Remember, it is not going to be easy, but if you don't try you will encounter many mental and/or physical illnesses over the course of your lifetime and maybe even die. I am sure most people don't want to die, so give yourself a chance to live and beat this disease. It's worth a try.

Steps That Can Help You Lose Weight

I wrote this book not only because I overcame anorexia but also because I was an anorexic who gained 62½ pounds by mistake and was able to lose it again. I am not anorexic anymore and I am not fat anymore. There are many books about how to lose weight. A summary of how an anorexic loses weight is different. The main thing to remember is that you have to love yourself and your body. When you love yourself, you treat yourself well. If you are too skinny or too fat, you are not treating yourself well. In fact, you are hurting yourself It's just as bad to be too fat as it is to be too skinny. A lot of fat people have high cholesterol and high blood pressure.

If you really want to lose weight, there are several things you can do:

1. Eat three regular meals a day. It is good to speak to a dietician who can plan those meals out for you. A dietician can really open your eyes to correct portion sizes too. It's a lot smaller than most people think.
2. Exercise whenever you can. Exercise definitely can help you get and stay slim. You can do cardiovascular or weight training. They are both great for you.
3. Ask for help from a friend or family member who is relatively thin. You can copy what they eat if it helps too. Try not to eat alone because you may tend to binge eat.
4. Drink green tea every day because apparently it helps you lose weight. Try to have it between meals when you feel hungry and it will curb your appetite for a little while.
5. Try not to eat bread or junk food (sweets) because they can put weight on you right away. Stick to salads, fish, chicken, fruits and meat.
6. Last, but most important, is that you have to want to lose weight. If you want to look better and be healthier, you have to try to lose weight. As I mentioned before, many overweight people have high cholesterol and high blood

pressure and many other illnesses. These can kill you just like being underweight can. Believe it or not, when I was fat for two years, my doctor told me I had high cholesterol. He threatened that if I didn't lower my cholesterol, he would put me on cholesterol pills for the rest of my life.

I overcame anorexia and being overweight at the same time and I feel great. I don't know if I did any further damage to myself but the body has an amazing ability to heal itself. I don't have high cholesterol anymore and I don't have bad skin or frizzy hair anymore either. Being anorexic or overweight is deadly, but if you really want to change, you can. You may have to suffer a little bit but the results speak for themselves.

Printed in the United States
49319LVS00006B/334

9 781424 120673